The best of all gifts around any Christmas tree:
the presence of a happy family all wrapped up in each other.

Family
Christmas
Songbook

Wise Publications
part of the Music Sales Group
London / New York / Paris / Sydney / Copenhagen / Madrid / Tokyo / Berlin

Exclusive distributors:

Music Sales Limited
8/9 Frith Street, London, W1D 3JB, England.

Music Sales Corporation
257 Park Avenue South, New York, NY10010,
United States of America.

Music Sales Pty Limited
120 Rothschild Avenue, Rosebery,
NSW 2018, Australia.

Order No. AM980716
ISBN 1-8444-9-636-8
This book © Copyright 2004 by
    Wise Publications.

Project editor: Heather Ramage.
Recipes by Alison Hedger.
Music processed by Jerry Lanning,
    Note-orious Productions Limited and Enigma.
Designed & art directed by Michael Bell Design.
Illustrated by Arlene Adams.

Your Guarantee of Quality:
As publishers, we strive to produce every book to the
highest commercial standards. The music has been carefully
designed to minimise awkward page turns and to make
playing from it a real pleasure. Particular care has been given
to specifying acid-free, neutral-sized paper made from
pulps which have not been elemental chlorine bleached.
This pulp is from farmed sustainable forests and was
produced with special regard for the environment.
Throughout, the printing and binding have been planned to
ensure a sturdy, attractive publication which should give years
of enjoyment. If your copy fails to meet our high standards,
please inform us and we will gladly replace it.

www.musicsales.com

Acknowledgements:
The editor and publishers gratefully acknowledge permission
to reproduce the following copyright material:

'Christmas Day' from The Country Child (Extract from
Chapter XII) by Alison Uttley. Reproduced by kind permission
of The Society of Authors as the Literary Representative of
the Estate of Alison Uttley.

'The Snow-man' by Mabel Marlowe. Reprinted by permission
of the author and Basil Blackwell (Publisher) Oxford.

'The Box Of Magic' by Malorie Blackman.
Copyright © Malorie Blackman, 1995. All Rights Reserved.
Reproduced by permission of Scholastic Limited.

The quote on page 1 is reprinted with permission from
Better Homes and Gardens Magazine.
Copyright © Meredith Corporation. All rights reserved.

Poems...

Stories...

Music...

Recipes...

Angels *From* The *Realms* Of *Glory*

 Words by **James Montgomery** *Music* **Traditional French**

Brightly

An - gels from the_ realms of glo - ry, wing your_ flight o'er_ all the earth;

ye who sang cre - a - tion's sto - ry now pro - claim Mes - si - ah's birth:

Family Christmas Songbook

Come_ _ _ and_ wor - ship

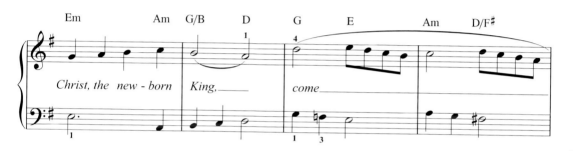

Christ, the new - born King,_ come_

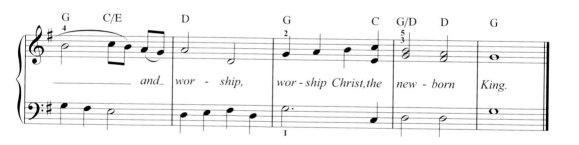

_ and_ wor - ship, wor - ship Christ,the new - born King.

2 Shepherds, in the field abiding,
Watching o'er your flocks by night,
God with us is now residing,
Yonder shines the infant light:
Come and worship...

3 Sages, leave your contemplations;
Brighter visions beam afar:
Seek the great Desire of Nations;
Ye have seen his natal star:
Come and worship...

4 Saints before the alter bending,
Watching long in hope and fear,
Suddenly the Lord, descending,
In His temple shall appear:
Come and worship...

5 Though an infant now we view Him,
He shall fill his Father's throne,
Gather all the nations to him;
Ev'ry knee shall then bow down:
Come and worship...

Away *In A Manger*

Words & Music by **William James Kirkpatrick**

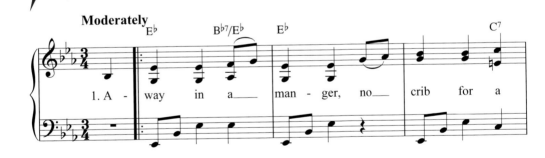

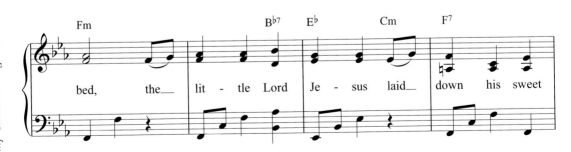

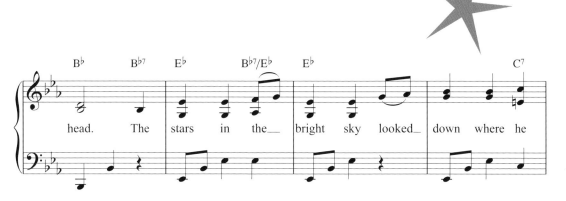

head. The stars in the__ bright sky looked_ down where he

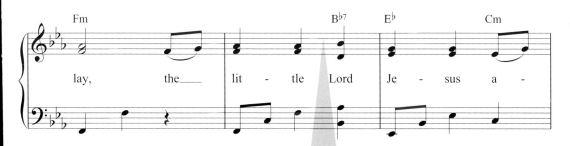

lay, the__ lit - tle Lord Je - sus a -

1. 2.   **3.**

poco rall.

sleep on the hay. 2. The   live with thee there.

2
The cattle are lowing, the baby awakes,
But little Lord Jesus no crying he makes.
I love thee, Lord Jesus! Look down from the sky,
And stay by my side until morning is nigh.

3
Be near me, Lord Jesus; I ask thee to stay
Close by me for ever, and love me, I pray.
Bless all the dear children in thy tender care,
And fit us for heaven, to live with thee there.

Away *In A Manger*

US Tune Words by ***William James Kirkpatrick*** *Music by* **James R Murray**

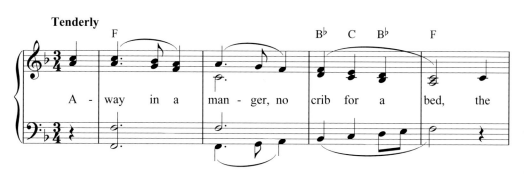

A - way in a man - ger, no crib for a bed, the

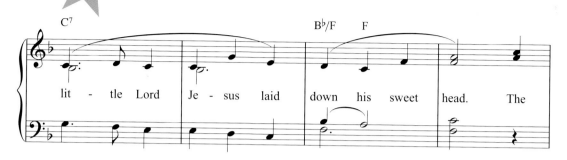

lit - tle Lord Je - sus laid down his sweet head. The

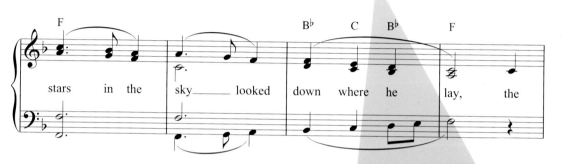

stars in the sky_____ looked down where he lay, the

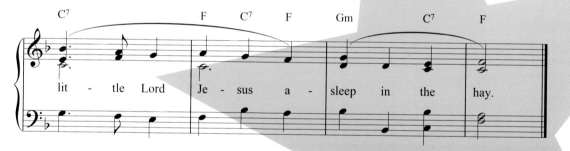

lit - tle Lord Je - sus a - sleep in the hay.

2 The cattle are lowing, the baby awakes,
But little Lord Jesus no crying he makes.
I love thee, Lord Jesus! Look down from the sky,
And stay by my side until morning is nigh.

3 Be near me, Lord Jesus; I ask thee to stay
Close by me for ever, and love me, I pray.
Bless all the dear children in thy tender care,
And fit us for heaven, to live with thee there.

Deck *The* Hall

Traditional Welsh

Brightly

Deck the hall with boughs of__ hol - ly, *fa la la la la la la la la.*

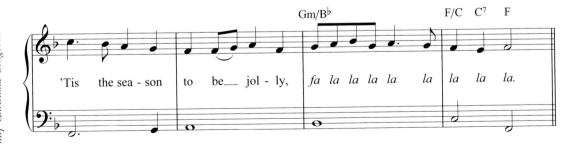

'Tis the sea - son to be__ jol - ly, *fa la la la la la la la la.*

Family Christmas Songbook

See the flowing bowl before us,
Fa la la la la la la la la,
Strike the harp and join the chorus,
Fa la la la la la la la la,
2 Follow me in merry measure,
Fa la la la la la la la la,
While I sing of beauty's treasure,
Fa la la la la la la la la la.

Fast away the old year passes,
Fa la la la la la la la la,
Hail the new, ye lads and lassies,
Fa la la la la la la la la,
3 Laughing, quaffing, all together,
Fa la la la la la la la la,
Heedless of the wind and weather.
Fa la la la la la la la la la.

Ding *Dong!* Merrily *On* High

Words by **George Ratcliffe Woodward** *Music* **Traditional French**

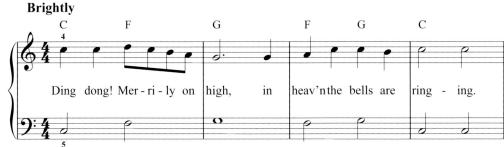

Ding dong! Mer-ri-ly on high, in heav'n the bells are ring-ing.

Ding dong! Ve - ri - ly the sky is riv'n with an - gels sing - ing.

Glo - - - - - - - - - - -

- - - - ri - a, ho - san - na in ex - cel - sis.

2
E'en so here below, below,
Let steeple bells be swungen,
And i-o, i-o, i-o,
By priest and people sungen.
Gloria, hosanna in excelsis…

3
Pray you, dutifully prime
Your matin chime, ye ringers;
May you beautifully rhyme
Your evetime song, ye singers.
Gloria, hosanna in excelsis…

The *First* Nowell

Traditional

Moderately

| D | Bm | A | Em/G | D/F♯ | G | D | G |

The_ first____ No - well the_ an - gel did say was to

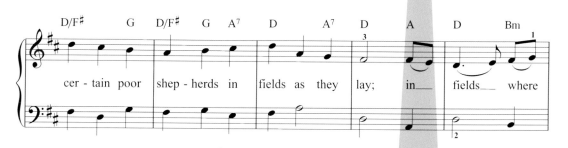

cer - tain poor | shep - herds in | fields as they | lay; | in___ | fields___ where

they | lay___ | keep - ing their | sheep, | on a | cold win - ter's | night___ that

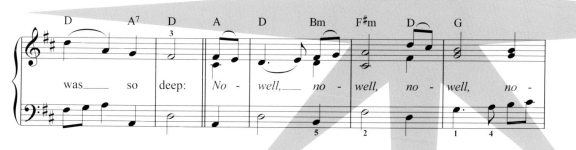

was___ | so | deep: | No - | well,___ | no - | well, | no - | well, | no -

well, | born is | the | King___ | of | Is - | ra - | el!

They lookèd up and saw a star,
2 Shining in the east, beyond them far,
And to the earth it gave great light,
And so it continued both day and night.
Nowell, Nowell…

And by the light of that same star,
3 Three wise men came from country far;
To seek for a king was their intent,
And to follow the star wherever it went.
Nowell, Nowell…

This star drew nigh to the north-west,
4 O'er Bethlehem it took its rest,
And there it did both stop and stay
Right over the place where Jesus lay.
Nowell, Nowell…

Then entered in those wise men three,
5 Full rev'rently upon their knee,
And offered there in his presence,
Their gold and myrrh and frankincense.
Nowell, Nowell…

Then let us all with one accord
6 Sing praises to our heav'nly Lord,
That hath made heav'n and earth of naught,
And with his blood mankind hath bought.
Nowell, Nowell…

Mr *Pickwick* On *The* Ice
by Charles *Dickens*

Mr Weller and the fat boy, having by their joint endeavours cut out a slide, were exercising themselves thereupon in a very masterly and brilliant manner. Sam Weller, in particular, was displaying that beautiful feat of fancy sliding which is currently denominated 'knocking at the cobbler's door', and which is achieved by skimming over the ice on one foot, and occasionally giving a two-penny postman's knock upon it with the other. It was a good long slide, and there was something in the motion which Mr Pickwick, who was very cold with standing still, could not help envying.

"It looks nice, warm exercise that, doesn't it?" he inquired of Wardle.

"Ah, it does indeed," replied Wardle. "Do you slide?"

"I used to do so, on the gutters, when I was a boy," replied Mr Pickwick.

"Try it now," said Wardle.

"Oh, do, please, Mr Pickwick!" cried all the ladies.

"I should be very happy to afford you any amusement," replied Mr Pickwick, "but I haven't done such a thing these thirty years."

"Pooh! Pooh! Nonsense!" said Wardle. "Here, I'll keep you company. Come along!"

And away went the good-tempered old fellow down the slide, with a rapidity which came very close upon Mr Weller, and beat the fat boy all to nothing.

Mr Pickwick paused, considered, pulled off his gloves and put them in his hat; took two or three short runs, balked himself as often, and at last took another run, and went slowly and gravely down the slide, with his feet about a yard and a quarter apart, amidst the gratified shouts of all the spectators.

"Keep the pot a-bilin', sir!" said Sam; and down went Wardle again, and then Mr Pickwick, and then Sam, and then Mr Winkle, and then Mr Bob Sawyer, and then the fat boy, and then Mr Snodgrass, following closely upon each other's heels, and running after each other with as much eagerness as if all their future prospects in life depended on their expedition.

It was the most intensely interesting thing to observe the manner in which Mr Pickwick performed his share in the ceremony; to watch the torture of anxiety

with which he viewed the person behind, gaining upon him at the imminent hazard of tripping him up; to see him gradually expend the painful force which he had put on at first, and turn slowly round on the slide, with his face towards the point from which he had started; to contemplate the playful smile which mantled on his face when he had accomplished the distance, and the eagerness with which he turned round when he had done so and ran after his predecessor – his black gaiters tripping pleasantly through the snow, and his eyes beaming cheerfulness and gladness through his spectacles. And when he was knocked down (which happened upon the average every third round), it was the most invigorating sight that can possibly be imagined to behold him gather up his hat, gloves, and handkerchief, with a glowing countenance, and resume his station in the rank with an ardour and enthusiasm that nothing could abate.

The sport was at its height, the sliding was at the quickest, the laughter was at the loudest, when a sharp, smart crack was heard. There was a quick rush towards the bank, a wild scream from the ladies, and a shout from Mr Tupman.

A large mass of ice disappeared; the water bubbled up over it; Mr Pickwick's hat, gloves, and handkerchief were floating on the surface; and this was all of Mr Pickwick that anybody could see.

Dismay and anguish were depicted on every countenance; the males turned pale, and the females fainted; Mr Snodgrass and Mr Winkle grasped each other by the hand, and gazed at the spot where their leader had gone down, with frenzied eagerness; while Mr Tupman, by way of rendering the promptest assistance, and at the same time conveying to any persons who might be within hearing the clearest possible notion of the catastrophe, ran off across the country at his utmost speed, screaming "Fire!" with all his might.

It was at this very moment, when old Wardle and Sam Weller were approaching the hole with cautious steps, and Mr Benjamin Allen was holding a hurried consultation with Mr Bob Sawyer on the advisability of bleeding the company generally, as an improving little bit of professional practice – it was at this very moment that a face, head, and shoulders emerged from beneath the water, and disclosed the features and spectacles of Mr Pickwick.

"Keep yourself up for an instant – for only one instant!" bawled Mr Snodgrass.

"Yes, do; let me implore you – for my sake!" roared Mr Winkle, deeply affected.

The adjuration was rather unnecessary – the probability being that if Mr Pickwick had declined to keep himself up for anybody else's sake, it would have occurred to him that he might as well do so for his own.

"Do you feel the bottom there, old fellow?" said Wardle.

"Yes, certainly," replied Mr Pickwick, wringing the water from his head and face, and gasping for breath. "I fell upon my back. I couldn't get on my feet at first."

The clay upon so much of Mr Pickwick's coat as was yet visible bore testimony to the accuracy of this statement; and as the fears of the spectators were still further relieved by the fat boy's suddenly recollecting that the water was nowhere more than five feet deep, prodigies of valour were performed to get him out. After a vast quantity of splashing, and cracking, and struggling, Mr Pickwick was at length fairly extricated from his unpleasant position, and once more stood on dry land.

"Oh, he'll catch his death of cold," said Emily.

"Dear old thing!" said Arabella. "Let me wrap this shawl round you, Mr Pickwick."

"Ah, that's the best thing you can do," said Wardle, "and when you've got it on, run home as fast as your legs can carry you, and jump into bed directly."

A dozen shawls were offered on the instant. Three or four of the thickest having been selected, Mr Pickwick was wrapped up, and started off, under the guidance of Mr Weller – presenting the singular phenomenon of an elderly gentleman, dripping wet, and without a hat, with his arms bound down to his sides, skimming over the ground, without any clearly-defined purpose, at the rate of six good English miles an hour.

But Mr Pickwick cared not for appearances in such an extreme case, and urged on by Sam Weller, he kept at the very top of his speed until he reached the door of Manor Farm, where Mr Tupman had arrived some five minutes before, and had frightened the old lady into palpitations of the heart by impressing her with the unalterable conviction that the kitchen chimney was on fire – a calamity which always presented itself in glowing colours to the old lady's mind when anybody about her evinced the smallest agitation.

Mr Pickwick paused not an instant until he was snug in bed.

Good *King* Wenceslas

Words by **J M Neale** *Music* **Traditional**

Moderately

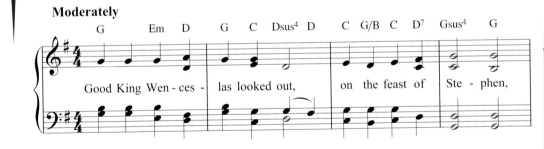

Good King Wen - ces - las looked out,   on the feast of   Ste - phen,

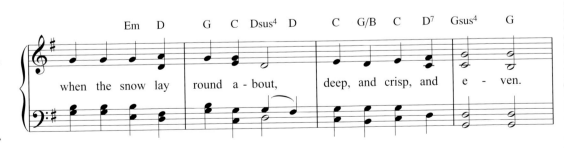

when the snow lay   round a - bout,   deep, and crisp, and   e - ven.

Family Christmas Songbook

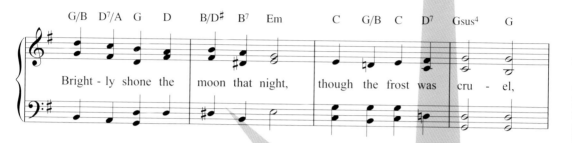

Bright - ly shone the | moon that night, | though the frost was | cru - el,

when a poor man | came in sight, | gath - 'ring win - ter | fu - el.

2
'Hither, page, and stand by me,
If thou know'st it, telling,
Yonder peasant, who is he,
Where and what his dwelling?'
'Sire, he lives a good league hence,
Underneath the mountain,
Right against the forest fence,
By Saint Agnes' fountain.'

3
'Bring me flesh, and bring me wine,
Bring me pine-logs hither:
Thou and I will see him dine,
When we bring them thither.'
Page and monarch, forth they went,
Forth they went together;
Through the rude wind's wild lament,
And the bitter weather.

4
'Sire, the night is darker now,
And the wind blows stronger;
Fails my heart, I know not how;
I can go no longer.'
'Mark my footsteps good, my page;
Tread thou in them boldly:
Thou shalt find the winter's rage
Freeze thy blood less coldly.'

5
In his master's steps he trod,
Where the snow lay dinted;
Heat was in the very sod
Which the Saint had printed.
Therefore, Christians all, be sure,
Wealth or rank possessing,
Ye who now will bless the poor,
Shall yourselves find blessing.

Hark! *The* Herald *Angels* Sing

Words by **Charles Wesley** *Music by* **Felix Mendelssohn**

Hark! The her - ald an - gels sing— glo - ry to the new - born King.

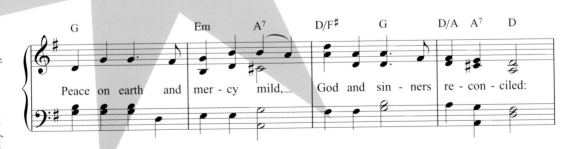

Peace on earth and mer - cy mild,— God and sin - ners re - con - ciled:

G/B · C · G/B · D⁷/F♯ · G · G/D · D · G/B · C · G/B · D⁷/F♯ · G · G/D · D

Joy - ful all ye na - tions rise,___ join the tri - umph of the skies,___

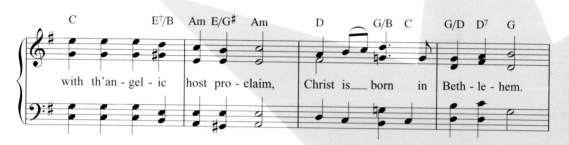

C · E⁷/B · Am E/G♯ · Am · D · G/B C · G/D D⁷ · G

with th'an - gel - ic host pro - claim, Christ is___ born in Beth - le - hem.

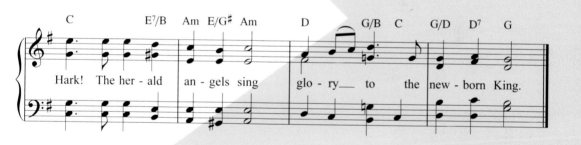

C · E⁷/B · Am E/G♯ Am · D · G/B C · G/D D⁷ · G

Hark! The her - ald an - gels sing glo - ry___ to the new - born King.

2

Christ, by highest heav'n adored,
Christ, the everlasting Lord,
Late in time behold him come,
Offspring of a Virgin's womb!
Veiled in flesh the Godhead see,
Hail, the incarnate Deity!
Pleased as man with us to dwell,
Jesus, our Emmanuel.
Hark! The herald angels sing etc…

3

Hail, the heav'n-born Prince of Peace!
Hail, the Sun of Righteousness!
Light and life to all he brings,
Ris'n with healing in his wings;
Mild he lays His glory by,
Born that we no more may die,
Born to raise us from the earth,
Born to give us second birth.
Hark! The herald angels sing etc…

The *Holly* And *The* Ivy

Traditional

Moderately

The hol - ly and the i - vy, when they are both full grown, of___

all the trees that are in the wood, the___ hol - ly bears the crown: *The*

Family Christmas Songbook

C   G   N.C.   C   D

ris - ing of the   sun___ and the   run - ning of   the   deer,   the___

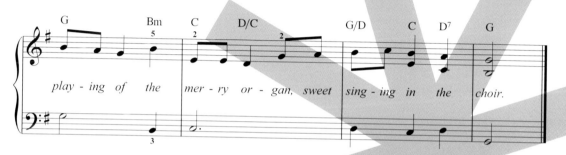

G   Bm   C   D/C   G/D   C   D⁷   G

play - ing of the   mer - ry or - gan, sweet   sing - ing in   the   choir.

2
The holly bears a blossom,
White as the lily flow'r,
And Mary bore sweet Jesus Christ
To be our sweet Saviour.
The rising of the sun…

3
The holly bears a berry,
As red as any blood,
And Mary bore sweet Jesus Christ
To do poor sinners good.
The rising of the sun…

4
The holly bears a prickle,
As sharp as any thorn,
And Mary bore sweet Jesus Christ
On Christmas Day in the morn.
The rising of the sun…

5
The holly bears a bark,
As bitter as any gall,
And Mary bore sweet Jesus Christ
For to redeem us all.
The rising of the sun…

6
The holly and the ivy,
When they are both full grown,
Of all the trees that are in the wood,
The holly bears the crown.
The rising of the sun…

I *Saw* Three *Ships*

Traditional

With a lilt

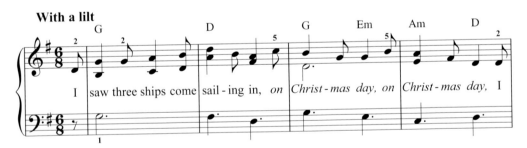

I saw three ships come sail-ing in, on Christ-mas day, on Christ-mas day, I

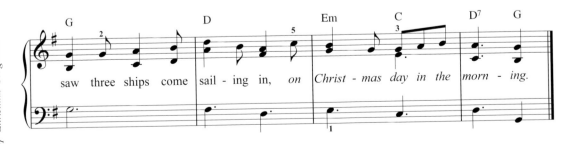

saw three ships come sail-ing in, on Christ-mas day in the morn-ing.

2 And what was in those ships all three?
On Christmas Day, on Christmas Day,
And what was in those ships all three?
On Christmas Day in the morning.

3 Our Saviour Christ and his lady.
On Christmas Day, on Christmas Day,
Our Saviour Christ and his lady.
On Christmas Day in the morning.

4 Pray, whither sailed those ships all three?
On Christmas Day, on Christmas Day,
Pray, whither sailed those ships all three?
On Christmas Day in the morning.

5 O, they sailed into Bethlehem.
On Christmas Day, on Christmas Day,
O, they sailed into Bethlehem.
On Christmas Day in the morning.

6 And all the bells on earth shall ring.
On Christmas Day, on Christmas Day,
And all the bells on earth shall ring.
On Christmas Day in the morning.

7 And all the angels in heaven shall sing.
On Christmas Day, on Christmas Day,
And all the angels in heaven shall sing.
On Christmas Day in the morning.

8 And all the souls on earth shall sing.
On Christmas Day, on Christmas Day,
And all the souls on earth shall sing.
On Christmas Day in the morning.

9 Then let us all rejoice amain!
On Christmas Day, on Christmas Day,
Then let us all rejoice amain!
On Christmas Day in the morning.

In *Dulci* Jubilo

English Words by **R L Pearsall** *Music Traditional*

Moderately

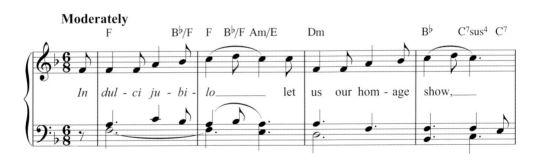

In dul - ci ju - bi - lo_____ let us our hom - age show,_____

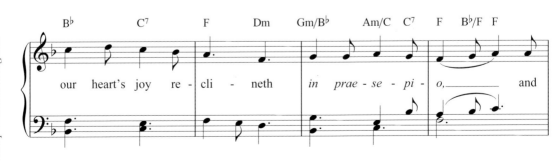

our heart's joy re - cli - neth in prae - se - pi - o,_____ and

Family Christmas Songbook

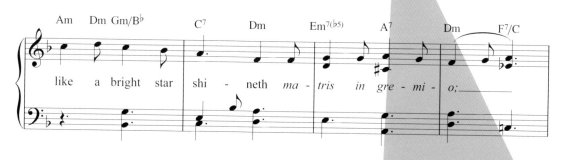

like a bright star shi - neth ma - tris in gre - mi - o;____

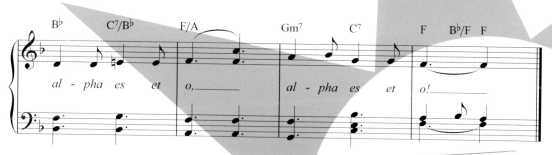

al - pha es et o,____ al - pha es et o!____

O Jesu parvule!
My heart is sore for thee!
Hear me, I beseech thee,
O puer optime!
My prayer let it reach thee
O Princeps gloriae!
Trahe me post te!
Trahe me post te!

2

O Patris caritas!
O nati lenitas!
Deep were we stainèd
Per nostra crimina;
But thou has for us gainèd
Coelorum gaudia:
O that we were there,
O that we were there!

3

Ubi sunt gaudia, where,
If that they be not there?
There, are angels singing
Nova cantica;
There the bells are ringing
In Regis curia:
O that we were there,
O that we were there!

4

O Come *All* Ye *Faithful*

Original Words & Music by **John Francis Wade**
English Words by **Frederick Oakeley**

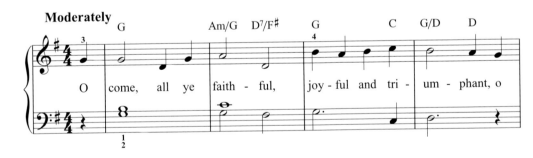

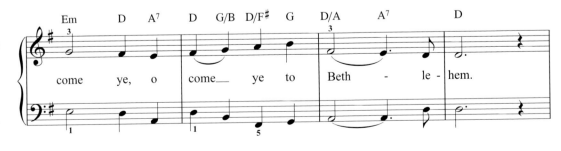

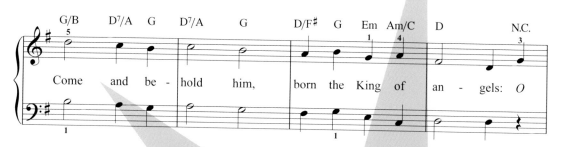

Come and be - hold him, born the King of an - gels: O

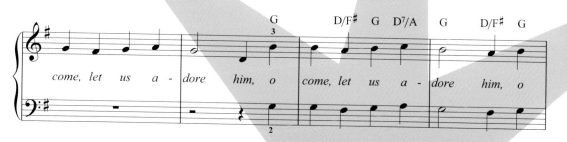

come, let us a - dore him, o come, let us a - dore him, o

come, let us a - dore him,___ Christ___ the Lord.

2
God of God,
Light of light,
Lo! He abhors not the Virgin's womb;
Very God, begotten, not created:
O come, let us adore him…

3
Sing choirs of angels,
Sing in exultation,
Sing all ye citizens of heav'n above;
Glory to God in the highest:
O come, let us adore him…

4
Yea, Lord, we greet thee,
Born this happy morning,
Jesu, to thee be glory giv'n;
Word of the Father, now in flesh appearing:
O come, let us adore him…

God *Rest* You *Merry,* Gentlemen

Traditional

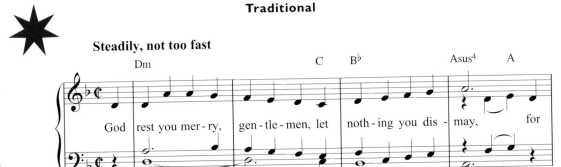

Steadily, not too fast

God rest you mer - ry, gen - tle - men, let noth - ing you dis - may, for

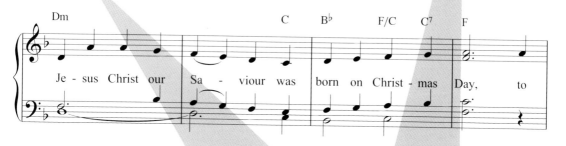

Je - sus Christ our Sa - viour was born on Christ - mas Day, to

save us all from Sa - tan's pow'r when we were gone a - stray

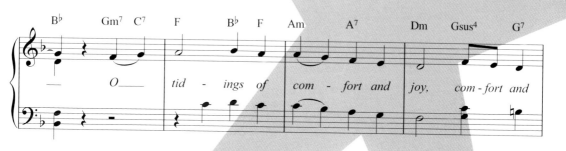

__ O___ tid - ings of com - fort and joy, com - fort and

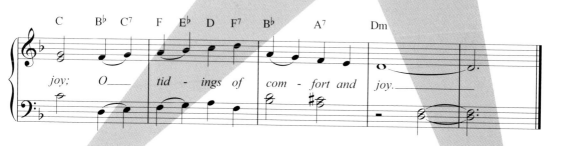

joy; O___ tid - ings of com - fort and joy.

2

In Bethlehem, in Jewry,
This blessèd babe was born,
And laid within a manger,
Upon this blessèd morn;
The which his mother Mary
Did nothing take in scorn.
O tidings of comfort and joy...

3 From God, our heav'nly Father,
A blessèd angel came,
And unto certain shepherds
Brought tidings of the same
How that in Bethlehem was born
The Son of God by name.
O tidings of comfort and joy…

4 'Fear not,' then said the angel,
'Let nothing you affright,
This day is born a Saviour,
Of virtue, pow'r and might;
By Him the world is overcome
And Satan put to flight.'
O tidings of comfort and joy…

5 The shepherds at those tidings
Rejoicèd much in mind,
And left their flocks a-feeding,
In tempest, storm and wind,
And went to Bethlehem straightway
This blessèd babe to find.
O tidings of comfort and joy…

6 But when to Bethlehem they came,
Whereat this infant lay,
They found him in a manger,
Where oxen feed on hay;
His mother Mary kneeling,
Unto the Lord did pray.
O tidings of comfort and joy…

7 Now to the Lord sing praises,
All you within this place,
And with true love and fellowship
Each other now embrace;
This holy tide of Christmas
All others doth deface.
O tidings of comfort and joy…

Christmas *Day* from '*The* Country *Child*' *by* Alison *Uttley*

Extract from Chapter XII

Susan awoke in the dark of Christmas morning. A weight lay on her feet, and she moved her toes up and down. She sat up and rubbed her eyes. It was Christmas Day. She stretched out her hands and found the knobby little stocking, which she brought into bed with her and clasped tightly in her arms as she fell asleep again. She awoke later and lay holding her happiness, enjoying the moment. The light was dim, but the heavy mass of the chest of drawers stood out against the pale walls, all blue like the snow shadows outside. She drew her curtains and looked out at the starry sky. She listened for the bells of the sleigh, but no sound came though the stillness except the screech owl's call.

Again she hadn't caught Santa Claus. Of course she knew he wasn't real, but also she knew he was. It was the same with everything. People said things were not alive but you knew in your heart they were: statues which would catch you if you turned your back were made of stone; Santa Claus was your own father and mother; the stuffed fox died long ago.

But suppose people didn't *know!* They hadn't seen that stone woman walk in Broomy Vale Arboretum, but she might, in the dark night. They hadn't seen Santa Claus and his sleigh, but that was because they were not quick enough. Susan had nearly caught things happening herself, she knew they only waited for her to go away. When she looked through a window into an empty room, there was always a guilty look about it, a stir of surprise.

Perhaps Santa Claus had left the marks of his reindeer and the wheels of his sleigh on the snow at the front of the house. She had never looked because last year there was no snow, and the year before she had believed in him absolutely. She would go out before breakfast, and perhaps she would find two marks of runners and a crowd of little hoof-marks.

She pinched the stocking from the toe to the top, where her white suspender tapes were stitched. It was full of nice knobs and lumps, and a flat thing like a book stuck out of the top. She drew it out – it was a book, just what she wanted most. She sniffed at it, and liked the smell of the cardboard back with deep letters cut in it. She ran her fingers along like a blind man and could not read the title, but there were three words in it.

Next came an apple, with its sweet, sharp odour. She recognised it, a yellow one, from the apple chamber, and from her favourite tree. She took a bite with her strong, white little teeth and scrunched it in the dark.

It was delicious fun, all alone, in this box-like room, with the dim blue-and-white jug on the washstand watching her, and the pool of the round mirror hanging on the wall, reflecting the blue dark outside, and the texts, "Thou God seest Me", and "Blessed are the Peace-makers", and "Though your sins be as scarlet they shall be white as wool". They could all see the things although she couldn't, and they were glad.

Next came a curious thing, pointed and spiked, with battlements like a tower. Whatever could it be? It was smooth like ivory and shone – even in the dark. She ran her fingers round the little rim and found a knob. She gave it a tug, and a ribbon flew out – it was a tape-measure to measure a thousand things, the trees' girths, the calf's nose, the pony's tail. She put it on her knee and continued her search.

There was a tin ball that unscrewed and was filled with comfits, and an orange, and a sugar mouse, all these were easy to feel, a sugar watch with a paper face and a chain of coloured ribbon, a doll's chair, and a penny china doll with a round smooth head. She at once named it Diana, after Diana of the Ephesians, for this one could never be an idol, being made of pot. She put her next to her skin down the neck of her nightdress, and pulled the last little bumps out of the stocking toe. They were walnuts, smelling of the orchards at Bird-in-Bush Farm, where they grew on great trees overhanging the wall, and a silver shilling, the only one she ever got, and very great wealth, but it was intended for the money-box in the hall.

It was the nicest Christmas stocking she had ever had, and she hugged her knees up to her chin and rocked with joy. Then she put her hand under her pillow and

brought out five parcels which had made five separate lumps under her head. They were quite safe.

She heard the alarm go off in her father's room and Dan's bell go jingle-jangle. Five o'clock, plenty of time yet before the hoof-marks would disappear. The wind swished softly against the window, and thumps and thuds sounded on the stairs. She slept again with the doll on her heart and the tape-measure under her cheek and the book in her hand.

A Child's Christmas Day
Anon

He opens his eyes with a cry of delight,
There's a toy-shop all round him, a wonderful sight!
The fairies have certainly called in the night.

They are quiet at first – both the girls and the boys,
Too happy to make any riot or noise,
And they mutually show to each other their toys.

Then Uncle appears with a smile on his lips,
As his fingers deep down in his pocket he dips,
A performance which ends in a series of 'tips'.

Next Sally brings pudding – the spirit burns blue,
They all dance around her, a merry young crew,
For they hope to eat mince-pie and plum-pudding too.

But, see! In the nursery a terrible racket,
The dolls lose their heads, there are rents in each jacket,
And if you've a toy, it's the fashion to crack it.

The floor is all littered with signs of the fray,
He is sulky and tired with much eating and play,
And Nurse too is cross as she bears him away.

O Little *Town* Of *Bethlehem*

Words by **Phillips Brooks** *Music* **Traditional**

At a moderate pace

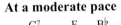

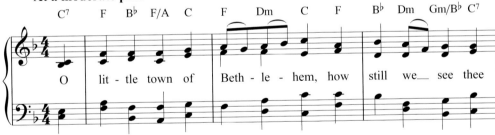

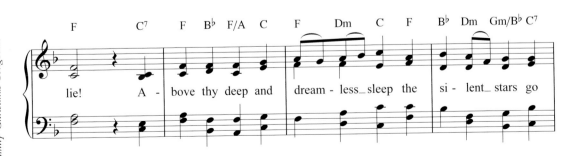

F   Am   B♭   C   F/A   Dm   C   C/B♭   F/A   Gm/B♭ G⁷/B

by.   Yet_   in   thy dark_ streets_ shi - neth the   ev - er - last - ing

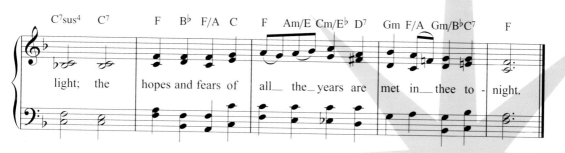

C⁷sus⁴   C⁷   F   B♭ F/A C   F   Am/E Cm/E♭ D⁷   Gm F/A Gm/B♭C⁷   F

light;   the   hopes and fears of   all_ the_ years are   met in_ thee to - night.

2
For Christ is born of Mary;
And, gathered all above,
While mortals sleep, the angels keep
Their watch of wond'ring love.
O morning stars, together
Proclaim the holy birth,
And praises sing to God the King,
And peace to men on earth!

3
How silently, how silently,
The wondrous gift is giv'n!
So God imparts to human hearts
The blessings of his heav'n.
No ear may hear his coming;
But in this world of sin,
Where meek souls will receive him, still
The dear Christ enters in.

4
O holy child of Bethlehem,
Descend to us, we pray;
Cast out our sin, and enter in,
Be born in us today.
We hear the Christmas angels
The great glad tidings tell:
O come to us, abide with us,
Our Lord Emmanuel.

O Little *Town* Of *Bethlehem*

US Tune Words by **Phillips Brooks** *Music by* **Lewis H Redner**

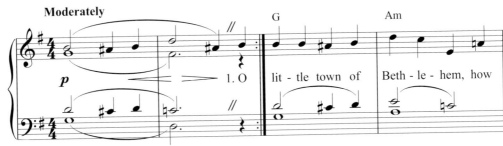

Family Christmas Songbook

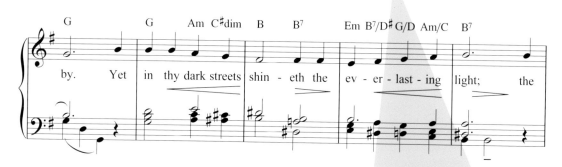

G   G   Am C#dim   B   B⁷   Em B⁷/D# G/D Am/C   B⁷

by.   Yet   in   thy dark streets   shin – eth the   ev - er - last - ing   light;   the

G   Am   C#dim G/B A⁷   D⁷ | 1. 2. 3. | 4.
                                     G   G

hopes and fears of   all   the years are   met   in   thee   to - night. 2.For   - el.
                                            (see block lyric)

2
For Christ is born of Mary;
And, gathered all above,
While mortals sleep, the angels keep
Their watch of wond'ring love.
O morning stars, together
Proclaim the holy birth,
And praises sing to God the King,
And peace to men on earth!

3
How silently, how silently,
The wondrous gift is giv'n!
So God imparts to human hearts
The blessings of his heav'n.
No ear may hear his coming;
But in this world of sin,
Where meek souls will receive him, still
The dear Christ enters in.

4
O holy child of Bethlehem,
Descend to us, we pray;
Cast out our sin, and enter in,
Be born in us today.
We hear the Christmas angels
The great glad tidings tell:
O come to us, abide with us,
Our Lord Emmanuel.

O Come, O Come, Emmanuel

Traditional English Words by **John Neale**

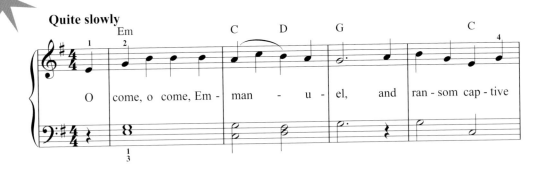

O come, o come, Em - man - u - el, and ran - som cap - tive

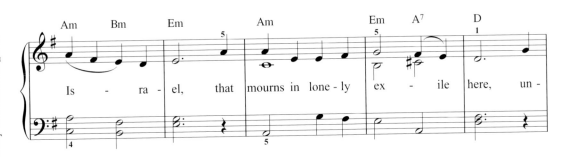

Is - ra - el, that mourns in lone - ly ex - ile here, un -

Family Christmas Songbook

til the Son of God_____ ap - pear. Re - joice! Re - joice! Em -

man - u - el shall come to thee, o Is - ra - el.

2
O come, thou rod of Jesse, free
Thine own from Satan's tyranny;
From depths of hell thy people save,
And give them vict'ry o'er the grave.
Rejoice! Rejoice!...

3
O come, thou dayspring, come and cheer
Our spirits by thine advent here;
Disperse the gloomy clouds of night,
And death's dark shadows put to flight.
Rejoice! Rejoice!...

4
O come, thou key of David, come,
And open wide our heav'nly home;
Make safe the way that leads on high,
And close the path to misery.
Rejoice! Rejoice!...

5
O come, o come, thou Lord of might,
Who to thy tribes, on Sinai's height
In ancient times didst give the Law
In cloud, and majesty and awe.
Rejoice! Rejoice!...

It Came Upon The Midnight Clear

Words by **Edmund Hamilton Sears** *Music* **Traditional**

It__ came up - on the__ mid - night clear, that glo - rious song__ of

old, from__ an - gels bend - ing near the earth to__ touch__ their harps of

Family Christmas Songbook

44

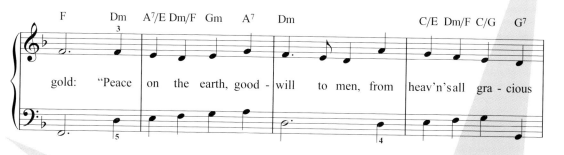

| F | Dm | A⁷/E Dm/F Gm | A⁷ | Dm | | C/E Dm/F C/G | G⁷ |

gold: "Peace │ on the earth, good - │will to men, from │heav'n's all gra - cious

| C | C⁷/B♭ | F/A Gm/B♭ D⁷ | | Gm F/A C | | B♭ Gm⁷ F/C C⁷ | F |

King!" The │world in so - lemn_ │still - ness lay to_ │ hear_ the an - gels │sing.

Still through the cloven skies they come,
With peaceful wings unfurled;
And still their heav'nly music floats
2 O'er all the weary world:
Above its sad and lowly plains
They bend on hov'ring wing;
And ever o'er its Babel-sounds
The blessèd angels sing.

Yet with the woes of sin and strife
The world has suffered long;
Beneath the angel-strain have rolled
3 Two-thousand years of wrong;
And warring humandkind hears not
The love-song which they bring:
O hush the noise of mortal strife,
And hear the angels sing!

And ye, beneath life's crushing load,
Whose forms are bending low,
Who toil along the climbing way
4 With painful steps and slow:
Look now! For glad and golden hours
Come swiftly on the wing;
O rest beside the weary road,
And hear the angels sing.

For lo, the days are hast'ning on,
By prophets seen of old,
When with the ever-circling years
5 Comes round the age of gold;
When peace shall over all the earth
Its ancient splendours fling,
And all the world give back the song
Which now the angels sing.

It Came Upon The Midnight Clear

US Tune Words by **Edmund Hamilton Sears** *Music by* *Richard Storrs Willis*

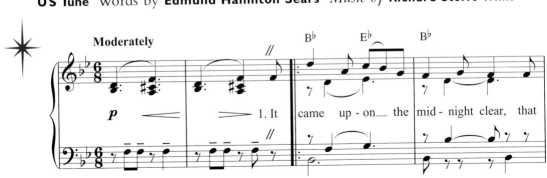

It Came Upon The Midnight Clear (US Tune)

2 Still through the cloven skies they come,
With peaceful wings unfurled;
And still their heav'nly music floats
O'er all the weary world:
Above its sad and lowly plains
They bend on hov'ring wing;
And ever o'er its Babel-sounds
The blessèd angels sing.

3 Yet with the woes of sin and strife
The world has suffered long;
Beneath the angel-strain have rolled
Two-thousand years of wrong;
And warring humandkind hears not
The love-song which they bring:
O hush the noise of mortal strife,
And hear the angels sing!

4 And ye, beneath life's crushing load,
Whose forms are bending low,
Who toil along the climbing way
With painful steps and slow:
Look now! For glad and golden hours
Come swiftly on the wing;
O rest beside the weary road,
And hear the angels sing.

5 For lo, the days are hast'ning on,
By prophets seen of old,
When with the ever-circling years
Comes round the age of gold;
When peace shall over all the earth
Its ancient splendours fling,
And all the world give back the song
Which now the angels sing.

Cooking *With* Mixed *Ages*

Have an adult in overall charge.

•

The recipes are suitable for involving ages 7 and upwards,
although very young family members can be involved with weighing,
washing vegetables, sifting, mixing, and tipping!

•

If children are helping, please be very aware of the hazards in a kitchen –
sharp knives, hot ovens and dishes, and wobbly stools and chairs.

•

Always assemble the ingredients and weigh them out before
beginning the recipe, and turn the oven on if needed.

•

For the sake of hygiene, all children's noses should be blown
and hands thoroughly washed before handling any of the ingredients
and participating in food preparations.

•

Aim to clear up as you go along. A tidy kitchen is a safer kitchen.

•

*The planning, preparing and cooking of food, followed by
eating it together is a time-honoured pastime and one which will
surely give your family a great deal of pleasure. Have fun!*

Winter *Turkey* & *Vegetable* Broth

Option: omit the turkey for a delicious vegetarian vegetable broth

175g (6oz) cold cooked turkey meat, cut into tiny pieces[*]

2 vegetable or chicken stock cubes dissolved in 855 millilitres (1$\frac{1}{2}$ pints) of hot water

A little olive oil

2 white onions, 2 carrots, 2 potatoes and 1 large stick of celery, prepared by washing, peeling and chopping

1 level teaspoon mild curry powder

30g (1oz) white flour *(plain or self-raising)*

1 heaped teaspoon mixed dried herbs

7g ($\frac{1}{4}$oz) in total of fresh parsley, basil or coriander, washed and chopped

115g (4oz) each of frozen sweet corn, frozen peas and frozen sliced green runner beans *(or any other frozen vegetables available)*

285 millilitres ($\frac{1}{2}$ pint) of light evaporated milk *(or use full cream regular milk)*

Salt and pepper to taste

Optional pinch of cayenne pepper

- Pour a little olive oil into a large saucepan, and add all the prepared FRESH vegetables. Mix in the curry powder and cook the vegetables on a medium heat for about 4 minutes, turning all the time with a wooden spoon.
- Remove from the heat and stir in the flour and gradually add the stock liquid, stirring as it is added.
- Add the chopped fresh herbs and return the pan to a slow heat, and cook for about half an hour with the saucepan lid on (cooking time will depend on the size of the vegetable pieces: smaller pieces will cook quicker than large chunks).
- Carefully add all the frozen vegetables and the cooked turkey pieces, replace the saucepan lid and continue to cook on a slow heat for 15 minutes.
- Remove the pan from the heat and add the evaporated milk and season the broth as required. Adults may care to sprinkle a little cayenne pepper on their portion of broth.

* If no left-over cooked turkey is available, cook two fresh turkey breasts in a little olive oil and cool thoroughly. Chop the turkey into tiny pieces. Proceed with the recipe as above. Do not leave warm cooked turkey standing at room temperature for too long – store in the refrigerator.

Christmas Greeting
Traditional

**Sing hey! Sing hey!
For Christmas Day;
Twine mistletoe and holly,
For friendship glows
In winter snows,
And so let's all be jolly.**

Fruits *Of* The *Forest* Compote

**1 Fruits of the Forest *(or any red fruit/berry)* tea bag
covered with 855 millilitres (1¹/₂ pints) of boiling water –
use a large jug and leave to infuse for 5 minutes**

2 teaspoons lemon juice

**1 tablespoon rose water *(you can find this in the
home-baking section at the supermarket)***

115g (4oz) caster sugar

5 sweet dessert apples
Option: firm dessert pears can be used to replace some or all of the apples

**230g (8oz) in total of mixed frozen fruit:
blackberries, raspberries, blueberries or cranberries**

- Remove the tea bag from the jug of freshly made fruit tea.
- Add the lemon juice and rose water to the infusion.
- Put the sugar into a large saucepan and pour the tea mixture into the pan.
- Stir well until all the sugar is dissolved.
- Quarter, peel and core the apples (or pears), slicing them into
slender pieces and add to the liquid in the pan.
- Gently heat and cook the fruit in the liquid on a medium heat
until the pieces are soft. (Do not boil furiously).
- Cool the pan of cooked fruit to room temperature, and add the frozen fruit.
- Turn the compote into an attractive serving bowl.

*The delicate, fruity flavour of this compote is delicious; the juice makes an
excellent drink! If keeping the compote for several hours, cover with cling film.
The taste will mature the longer the berries (especially blackberries) are left in the liquid.*

Bubbling
Apple & Bread Pudding

4 cooking or dessert apples

Bowl of cool water with a large squeeze of lemon juice stirred in

75g (2^1/$_2$oz) bread *(fresh or stale, white or brown)* with crusts removed

60g (2oz) whole rolled porridge oats

60g (2oz) juicy raisins

75g (2^1/$_2$oz) soft brown sugar

240-300 millilitres (8-10 fluid oz) milk *(more if the bread is very stale)*

Bowl of Muscovado sugar, to add individually, to taste

- Quarter and peel the apples one at a time, and remove the core.
- Chop the four quarters into small pieces and put the bits into the lemon water to stop them from discolouring.
- Slice the bread and then pull with fingers into small chunks, roughly 1 cm square.
- Put the oats and raisins into a large bowl and add the bread, drained apples and soft brown sugar. Mix up thoroughly.
- Pour on the milk and stir, leaving for 5 minutes so that the liquid is almost all soaked into the bread.
(Use enough milk, otherwise the pudding won't bubble).
- Tip the mixture into an oven proof oven-to-table dish and place in a moderate oven for about 25–30 minutes. (350°F, 177°C, gas mark 4).

The Apple and Bread Pudding should be bubbling and golden brown with crusty golden pieces of bread and oats on the surface.
Serve hot, with fresh cream, custard or ice cream, and a bowl of Muscovado sugar to be sprinkled as individually desired.

Christmas *Fruit* Cake

No eggs or butter!
Lower in cholesterol and saturated fat than usual Christmas cake.

75g (2^1/2oz) each of raisins, sultanas, currants and
quartered glace cherries

60g (2oz) ready-preserved chopped mixed peel

15g (^{1}/2 oz) chopped stem ginger removed from storage syrup

Finely grated rind of 1 lemon and 1 orange *(scrub fruit well if waxed)*

250 millilitres (8 fluid oz) of fruit juice *(apple or orange)*

15g (^{1}/2oz) sunflower seeds *(or pumpkin seeds)*

30g (1oz) broken nuts *(blanched almonds, walnuts, hazel or pecan nuts)*

115 grams (4oz) Muscovado sugar

60 millilitres (2 fluid oz) delicately flavoured cooking oil
(grapeseed, sweet almond or sunflower)

90 millilitres (3 fluid oz) milk

30 millilitres (1 fluid oz) other liquid – more milk,
fruit juice, brandy or rum

225g (8oz) self-raising white flour

2 heaped teaspoons mixed spice

• Soak the raisins, sultanas, currants, cherries, preserved mixed peel, ginger and fresh lemon and orange rinds, overnight in the fruit juice. Use a large mixing bowl big enough to eventually take all the other ingredients.

• Add the seeds, nuts and Muscovado sugar to the mixture. Stir well.

• Stir in the oil, milk and other liquid. Mix thoroughly.

• Sift the flour and spice, and gradually add it to the mixture, stirring as you go. The mixture should drop easily from the spoon.

• Tip the cake mixture into a round, non-stick cake tin with a loose bottom; size 19.75cm x 9.25cm (7$\frac{1}{2}$ inch x 3$\frac{5}{8}$ inch).

• Cook for 1$\frac{1}{2}$ hours in a slow oven (150°F, 65°C, gas mark 2) until the cake is firm to the touch. Pierce the cake with a sharp knife to see if the blade is free of uncooked mixture when removed. If not, pop the cake back in the oven until cooked.

• When cooked turn out and cool on a wire rack. Do not cover until completely cool. Store in an air tight tin.

SCRUMPTIOUS – but try to wait until the next day to eat the cake!

Option: cover with marzipan and icing in the usual Christmas cake tradition.

For The Children Or The Grown-ups?

Anon

'Tis the week before Christmas and every night
As soon as the children are snuggled up tight
And have sleepily murmured their wishes and prayers,
Such fun as goes on in the parlour downstairs!
For Father, Big Brother, and Grandfather too,
Start in with great vigour, their youth to renew.
The grown-ups are having great fun – all is well;
And they play till it's long past their hour for bed.

They try to solve puzzles and each one enjoys
The magical thrill of mechanical toys,
Even Mother must play with a doll that can talk,
And if you assist it, it's able to walk.
It's really no matter if paint may be scratched,
Or a cogwheel, a nut, or a bolt gets detached;
The grown-ups are having great fun – all is well;
The children don't know it, and Santa won't tell.

Mincemeat &
Marshmallow *Melts*

Plain digestive biscuits

White marshmallows

Mincemeat

- Thinly spread each biscuit with mincemeat.
- Place one marshmallow in the centre of the spread biscuit.
- Microwave at full power for 20 seconds maximum.

Beware: the melt will be very hot at first. This is a super-sweet treat!

Santa's *Ice* Cream *Soda*

Soft scoop vanilla ice cream

**Cream soda *(You will find this in the soft drinks
section at the supermarket)***

- Pour ½ glass of cream soda.
- Add a generous scoop of ice cream.
- Serve with festive Christmas straws, standing on
a tray bedecked with tinsel.

Christmas *Trifle*

175g (6oz) Madeira cake

Raspberry or strawberry jam

285 millilitres ($^1/_2$ pint) creamy milk

1 banana

Handful of blanched, split almonds

570 millilitres (1 pint) ready made full cream custard

60g (2oz) fresh raspberries *(or well drained tinned or thawed frozen raspberries)*

430 millilitres ($^3/_4$ pint) whipped double cream

Sprig of plastic holly

• Break the cake into small pieces and put them into a large serving bowl.
• Drop lots of large blobs of jam on top of the cake.
• Carefully pour the milk over the cake and allow the liquid to be absorbed.
(The cake should be thoroughly wetted, but not swimming.
Adjust the milk needed according to the cake you are using).
• Peel the banana and thinly slice. Place the slices evenly over the soaked cake.
• Sprinkle the almonds over the banana.
• Cover everything with the custard.
• Place the raspberries over the custard.
• Spread the whipped cream over the raspberries.
• Just before serving, sprinkle the top with more almonds if you have
some left, and stick the sprig of plastic holly in the centre.

Sans *Day* Carol

Traditional

Quite lively

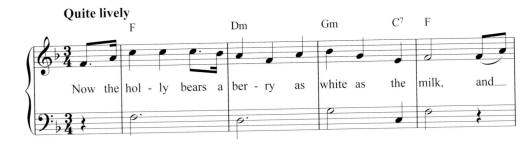

Now the hol- ly bears a ber- ry as white as the milk, and__

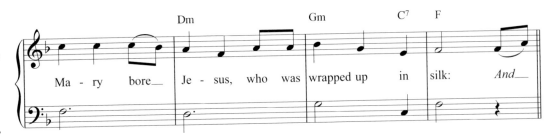

Ma- ry bore__ Je- sus, who was wrapped up in silk: *And__*

Family Christmas Songbook

Ma - ry bore_ | Je - sus Christ our | Sa - viour for to | be, and the

first tree in the | green - wood, it | was the hol - ly, | hol - ly, hol -

- ly! And the | first tree in the | green - wood, it | was the hol - ly!

2 Now the holly bears a berry as green as the grass,
And Mary bore Jesus, who died on the cross:
And Mary bore...

3 Now the holly bears a berry as black as the coal,
And Mary bore Jesus who died for us all:
And Mary bore...

4 Now the holly bears a berry, as blood it is red,
Then trust we our saviour who rose from the dead:
And Mary bore...

O Christmas *Tree* (O Tannenbaum)

Traditional

Moderately

O Christ-mas tree, o Christ-mas tree! How true you stand un - chang - ing. O

Family Christmas Songbook

Christ - mas tree, o Christ - mas tree! How true you stand un - chang - ing. Your

boughs so green in sum - mer - time, re - main so green in win - ter - time. O

Christ - mas tree, o Christ - mas tree! How true you stand un - chang - ing!

2

O Christmas Tree, O Christmas Tree!
Thou hast a wonderous message.
O Christmas Tree, O Christmas Tree!
Thou hast a wonderous message.
Thou dost proclaim the Saviour's birth,
Goodwill to men and peace on earth.
O Christmas Tree, O Christmas Tree!
Thou hast a wonderous message.

Infant *Holy*, Infant *Lowly*

Traditional Polish

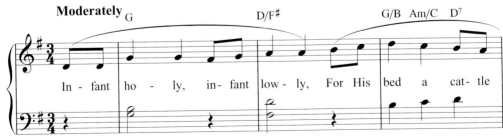

Moderately

In- fant ho - ly, in- fant low-ly, For His bed a cat- tle

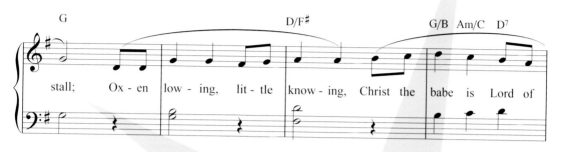

stall; Ox - en low - ing, lit - tle know - ing, Christ the babe is Lord of

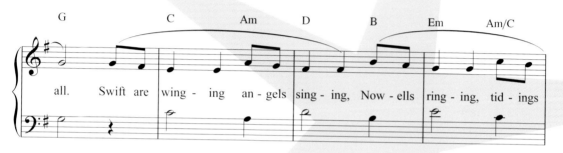

all. Swift are wing - ing an - gels sing - ing, Now - ells ring - ing, tid - ings

bring - ing, Christ the babe is Lord of all, Christ the babe is Lord of all.

2

Flocks were sleeping, shepherds keeping
Vigil 'til the morning new,
Saw the glory, heard the story,
Tidings of a gospel true.
Thus rejoicing, free from sorrow,
Praises voicing, greet the morrow,
Christ the babe was born for you,
Christ the babe was born for you.

Once *In* Royal *David's* City

Words by **Cecil Alexander** *Music by* **Henry Gauntlett**

Moderately slow

Once in roy - al Da - vid's ci - ty stood a low - ly cat - tle -

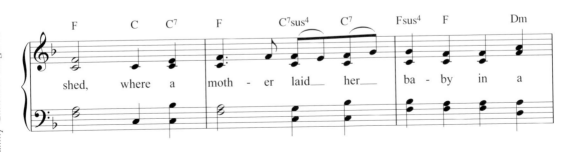

shed, where a moth - er laid___ her___ ba - by in a

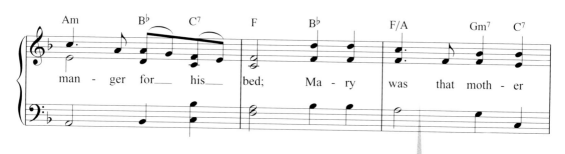

man - ger for__ his__ bed; Ma - ry was that moth - er

mild, Je - sus Christ her lit - tle__ child.

He came down to earth from heaven,
Who is God and Lord of all,
2 And his shelter was a stable,
And his cradle was a stall;
With the poor and mean and lowly,
Lived on earth our Saviour holy.

And through all his wondrous childhood
He would honour and obey,
3 Love and watch the lowly maiden,
In whose gentle arms he lay;
Christian children all must be
Mild, obedient, good as He.

For He is our childhood's pattern,
Day by day like us he grew,
4 He was little, weak and helpless,
Tears and smiles like us he knew;
And he feeleth for our sadness,
And he shareth in our gladness.

And our eyes at last shall see him
Through his own redeeming love,
5 For that child so dear and gentle
Is our Lord in heaven above;
And he leads his children on
To the place where he is gone.

Not in that poor lowly stable,
With the oxen standing by,
6 We shall see him; but in heaven,
Set at God's right hand on high;
Where like stars his children crowned
All in white shall wait around.

Joy *To* The *World*

Words by **Isaac Watts**   *Music by* **George Frideric Handel**

Joy to the world! The Lord is come; let earth re-

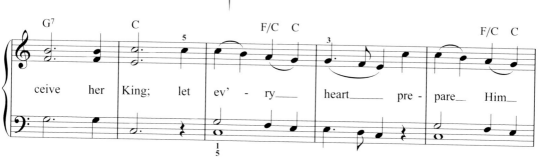

ceive her King; let ev' - ry___ heart___ pre - pare___ Him___

room,___ and heav'n and na - ture_ sing, and_ heav'n and na - ture_

sing, and_ hea - ven, and hea - ven and na - ture sing.

2 Joy to the earth! The Saviour reigns;
Let us our songs employ;
While fields and floods, rocks, hills and plains
Repeat the sounding joy,
Repeat the sounding joy,
Repeat, repeat the sounding joy.

3 He rules the world with truth and grace,
And makes the nations prove
The glories of his righteousness,
And wonders of his love,
And wonders of his love,
And wonders, and wonders of his love.

Jingle *Bells*

Words & Music by **J S Pierpont**

Brightly

Dash - ing through the snow in a one - horse o - pen sleigh,

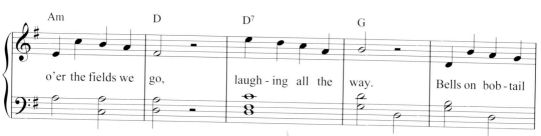

o'er the fields we go, laugh - ing all the way. Bells on bob - tail

Jingle Bells

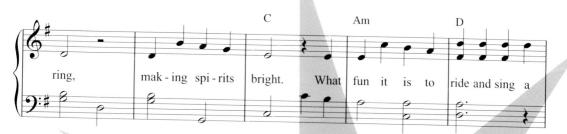

ring, mak - ing spi - rits bright. What fun it is to ride and sing a

sleigh - ing song to - night! *Oh!* *Jin - gle bells,* *jin - gle bells,* *jin - gle all the*

way. *Oh, what fun it* *is to ride in a* *one - horse o - pen* *sleigh! Oh!*

Jin - gle bells, jin - gle bells, jin - gle all the way.

Oh, what fun it is to ride in a one - horse o - pen sleigh!

2

Now the ground is white,
Go it while you're young.
Take the girls tonight,
Sing this sleighing song.
Get a bob-tailed bay,
Two-forty for his speed,
Then hitch him to an open sleigh
And crack! You'll take the lead.
Oh! Jingle bells…

The *Box* Of *Magic*
by *Malorie* Blackman

It was Christmas Eve, but Peter was in no hurry. His head bent, Peter dragged his feet as he made his way slowly home. There was no point in rushing. Mum and Dad would only be arguing about something or another. Peter and his sister Chloe had hoped that the quarrelling would stop over Christmas. It hadn't. If anything, it'd got worse.

Peter had spent all afternoon searching and searching for the perfect present for his Mum and Dad. Something that would stop them quarrelling for just five minutes. Something that would make Christmas the way it used to be, with smiles and songs and happiness in every corner of the house. But all the searching had been for nothing. Peter didn't have that much money to begin with and all the things he could afford, he didn't want. All the gifts he could afford looked so cheap and tacky that Peter knew they would fall apart about ten seconds after they were handled. What was he going to do? He had to buy something and time was running out.

Then he caught sight of it out of the corner of his eye. The medium-sized sign above the door said 'THE CHRISTMAS SHOP' in spidery writing. The small shop window was framed with silver and gold tinsel and a scattering of glitter like mini stars. At the bottom of the window, fake snow had been sprayed. It looked so much like the real thing that had it been outside the window instead of inside, Peter would've been sure it was real snow. A single Christmas tree, laden down with fairy lights and baubles and yet more tinsel, stood proudly in the exact centre of the window.

Peter stood in front of the shop and stared. He'd never seen anything so… wonderful! It was as if Christmas had started in this shop and then spread out to cover the whole wide world.

"The Christmas Shop…" Peter muttered to himself.

He wondered why he'd never seen it before. True, it was behind the shopping precinct and he usually walked through the precinct not around it, but even so. Peter looked up and down the street. The few other shops in the same row as

The Christmas Shop were all boarded up.

Unexpectedly, the shop door opened. A tall portly man with a white beard and a merry twinkle in his eyes stood in the doorway.

"Hello! Come in! Come in!" the shopkeeper beckoned.

"I ...er...don't have much money."

Peter shook his head.

"No matter. Come in."

The shopkeeper turned and held the door open. It was as if there was no doubt in his mind that Peter would enter. Uncertainly, Peter dithered on the pavement. He hadn't intended to go in. He was only window shopping. But the shop looked so warm and inviting and the shopkeeper seemed so friendly. Peter walked into the shop. And he gasped in amazement!

It was even better inside than it had appeared from outside. It smelt of freshly baked bread and warm cakes and toast and cinnamon and nutmeg and it was so warm; it was as if the sun itself had come for a visit.

"Isn't my shop the best!" smiled the shopkeeper. "Look around. Feel free. You can pick up anything, touch anything."

Peter stared at the shopkeeper. He certainly wasn't like any other shopkeeper Peter had ever met. Usually shopkeepers didn't like school kids in their shops and they certainly didn't like them touching things. Peter wandered around the shop, his dark brown eyes wide with delight. Toys and games and Christmas sweets and Christmas treats filled every corner.

Peter's hand curled around the money in his pocket. He could buy all his Christmas presents in here. Peter bent his head to examine a gold and berry-red scarf. That would be perfect for his mum. And maybe the night-blue and yellow scarf for his dad. And he could get that little glass unicorn over there for Chloe. That was just the kind of thing she liked. The strange thing was, none of the items had prices on them.

"H-How much are these woolly scarves?" Peter asked, crossing his fingers in his pockets. "And how much is that unicorn over there?"

"That depends on who they're for and why you think they'd like them," answered the shopkeeper.

"The scarves are for my Mum and Dad and the unicorn is for my sister. Chloe likes things made of glass. She keeps them in her bedroom on the window-sill. And I thought that Mum and Dad could have the scarves to keep them warm."

"And how much money do you have?" asked the shopkeeper.

Peter took out all the money in his pocket. The shopkeeper checked through it carefully.

"You're lucky," said the shopkeeper. "You've got enough for all the things you want."

"I have? Really?" Peter couldn't believe it.

The shopkeeper smiled and nodded. Peter grinned at him, but slowly his smile faded. He'd buy the scarves for his Mum and Dad and then what? What good would any present do? Peter could see it now. Mum and Dad opening their presents on Christmas Day.

"Thanks Peter. That's great," says Dad.

"Peter, that's wonderful," says Mum.

And then they'd fling their presents to the back of the chair and start shouting at each other again.

"What's the matter, Peter?" asked the shopkeeper gently.

Peter jumped. He'd been lost in a world of his own.

"It's just that ... Hang on a second. How did you know my name?" Peter stared.

"It's a little game of mine," the shopkeeper beamed. "I like to guess people's names, and nine times out of ten, I get it right."

Peter was impressed.

"So you were saying?" the shopkeeper prompted.

"I...I don't suppose you've got anything in your shop to stop my Mum and Dad from fighting?"

The moment the words were out of his mouth, Peter regretted it. What was he doing? He hadn't told anyone about his Mum and Dad, not even his best friend Andy. No one knew how things were at home except his sister Chloe, and she didn't talk about it either.

"Oh, I see. Do your Mum and Dad argue a lot?" asked the shopkeeper.

"All the time," Peter sighed.

The shopkeeper pursed his lips.

"Hhmm! I think I have just the present you need – for your whole family."

The shopkeeper went around his brightly coloured counter and disappeared down behind it. Moments later he straightened up, a huge smile on his face and a silver box in his hands.

"These are what you need," he said.

"What are they?" Peter asked doubtfully.

"Christmas crackers," announced the shopkeeper proudly. At the disappointed look on Peter's face, he added, "Ah, but they're not just any crackers. They're magic. Guaranteed to work, or your money back."

"How are they magic?" Peter asked suspiciously.

"The magic only works if they're pulled on Christmas Day, when you're all around the table eating dinner," explained the shopkeeper.

"But how do they work?"

"It's hard to explain. You have to see the magic for yourself."

"How much are they?" asked Peter, still doubtful. Maybe he could buy them and still get the other presents as well.

"I'm afraid they're very expensive because they're magic," said the shopkeeper. "They'll cost you all the money you've got, and even then I'm letting you have them cheap."

Peter thought for a moment. Magic crackers. Crackers that would actually stop Mum and Dad from arguing. They were worth the money if they could do that. He took a deep breath.

"All right, I'll take them," he said quickly, before he could change his mind.

Peter handed over his money and the shopkeeper handed over the box of eight crackers. Moments later, Peter was out of the shop and running all the way home. Magic crackers! He couldn't wait for Christmas Day.

"I've been in that kitchen since seven o'clock this morning. I think the least you could do is sit at the table with the rest of your family." Mum's voice dripped with ice.

"I want to watch the end of this film," Dad argued.

"Typical! You're so selfish," Mum snapped.

Peter and Chloe looked at each other and sighed. Mum and Dad were at it again. Christmas Day – and they were still arguing.

"Dad, you and Mum and Chloe can open my present now," Peter said desperately. "The man in The Christmas Shop said they should only be opened when we're all sitting round the table eating dinner."

"Oh, all right then," Dad grumbled.

"Oh, I see. You'll come to the table if Peter asks you to, but not if I ask you," sniffed Mum.

"Peter doesn't nag me every two seconds," Dad said as he sat down at the table.

Chloe shook her head and turned to look out of the window. Peter ran to get the present he'd bought. It was the only one left unopened under the tree. He stood between his Mum and Dad, putting the present down on the tablecloth. Mum and Dad looked at each other.

"Go on then," Dad prompted.

"You do it," said Mum.

"I'll do it," said Chloe. She tore off the bright red and yellow wrapping paper. "It's a box of crackers," she said, surprised.

"Not just any crackers," Peter said eagerly. "They're magic crackers!"

"Who told you that?" Mum smiled.

"The man in The Christmas Shop," Peter replied.

"Well, let's all sit down. Then we can pull them and get on with our dinner," said Dad, adding under his breath, "And maybe then I can get back to my film."

But the moment they all sat down, something peculiar began to happen. A strange feeling settled over the dinner table. A hopeful, expectant feeling – as if, in spite of themselves, everyone was waiting for something terrific, amazing and spectacular to happen all at once. The noise from the telly was just a distant hum at the other end of the room. Light, like warm spring sunshine, came from everyone, smiling at everyone else as they watched Dad place two crackers beside each plate. Chloe held out her cracker to Dad. Peter held his Christmas cracker out to Mum.

"One! Two! Three!" they all shouted.

Bang! Pop! The sound of exploding crackers filled the room. Chloe and Peter got the biggest parts of the crackers. They both peered down into them.

"They're...they're empty!" Chloe exclaimed.

"No! They can't be," frowned Mum.

"See for yourself," said Chloe, handing over her cracker.

Peter couldn't believe it. Empty...When he remembered the smiling, friendly face of the jolly man with the white beard in The Christmas Shop, he just couldn't believe it. That man wouldn't take his money and sell him a box of nothing – Peter was sure he wouldn't. And yet...and yet, his cracker was empty. Just an empty roll covered with some glossy paper and nothing else. No hats. No jokes. No gifts. Nothing.

"Maybe there were just two duff ones in the box," Mum suggested.

Mum and Dad pulled their crackers next. The same thing happened. They were empty. Chloe and Peter pulled crackers five and six at the same time as Mum and Dad pulled crackers seven and eight.

They were all empty.

Peter examined each one, hoping against hope that they'd got it wrong or it was a trick – but it wasn't. Peter looked at Chloe, then Mum and Dad – and burst into tears. He couldn't help it.

"The shopkeeper told me they were magic crackers," Peter sobbed to Mum and Dad. "I only bought them because he said they would make you stop arguing with each other. He promised me they were magic. He *promised* me..."

Dad stared. Mum's mouth fell open.

"You...you bought them – because of us?" Dad asked, aghast.

Peter sniffed and nodded.

"Never mind, Peter." Chloe put her arm around her younger brother's shoulder. "Besides, nothing would stop Mum and Dad from fighting. Not even a real box of magic crackers."

And with that, Chloe burst into tears too.

"Chloe! Peter!" Mum and Dad ran around the table to hug Peter and Chloe to them. "We had no idea we were quarrelling that much."

"And we had no idea we were upsetting both of you so much," said Dad.

But Peter and Chloe couldn't stop crying.

"I'll tell you what," said Mum. "Let's make our own Christmas crackers. All this food will stay warm in the oven until we've finished."

"Terrific idea."

Dad went over to the telly and switched it off.

"We'll make the hats first," Dad continued, "Out of newspaper."

Dad and Mum showed Peter and Chloe how to make sailor hats out of newspaper. That took about five minutes. Then they all sat down for dinner. Over dinner, everyone had to tell the worst jokes they knew, like, 'How do you make an apple puff? Chase it round the garden!' and 'Why did the elephant cross the road? Because it was the chicken's day off!'

Dad's joke was 'Why did silly Billy stand on a ladder when he was learning to sing? So he could reach the high notes!' And Mum's joke was ancient but she was still proud of it! 'How do you make a Swiss Roll? Push him down a hill!' Chloe told a joke that Peter didn't get until Mum explained it. 'How do you tell how old a telephone is? Count its rings!' (Mum explained that you could tell the age of a tree by counting the rings through its trunk.) Everyone got Peter's joke. 'Why are vampires crazy? Because they're often bats!' And when anyone ran out of jokes, they made them up, which was even funnier!

After dinner when everyone was eating Christmas pudding, Mum grabbed Dad and whispered in his ear. Suddenly they both dashed off upstairs with the empty crackers. Ten minutes later they reappeared with the various ends of each cracker now glued together.

"Cracker time!" said Mum. And she held out a cracker to Chloe.

They both pulled.

"POP!" shouted Mum.

Chloe looked inside the cracker and there was one of Mum's old bangles – the gold and blue one which had always been Chloe's favourite.

"Your turn," said Dad, holding out a cracker to Peter. They both shouted, "BANG!"

Peter looked inside the cracker. There was a pig made of Lego bricks. At least, that's what Peter thought it was.

"It's not a pig. It's a rocket!" said Dad indignantly.

Mum started to giggle.

"I told you it looked more like a pig, dear," she said.

They 'popped' the rest of the crackers. They all had very silly, very tacky, very wonderful presents in them.

"Who needs rotten, mouldy old crackers?" asked Dad. "We can do it all ourselves."

"And they're much better too," Mum agreed. "It's just a shame that Peter got conned out of his money. Where did you say the shop was?"

"Behind the precinct. All the other shops on the same street were boarded up," Peter replied.

"There aren't any shops behind the precinct. The last one closed down over a year ago," Dad frowned.

"There's one still open. It's called The Christmas Shop," said Peter.

Mum and Dad looked at each other. They both shrugged.

"Never mind. I'd say they were the best crackers we've ever had," smiled Mum. "My jaw still aches from laughing at all those terrible jokes."

"Those crackers were...a box of magic," said Dad, giving Mum a cuddle.

Later that night, as Peter lay in bed, he still couldn't quite believe what had happened. Mum and Dad hadn't argued once since the crackers had been pulled. In fact, it was the most wonderful day they'd all had in a long, long time. The only cloud was the shopkeeper who'd sold Peter the crackers in the first place. Peter still didn't want to believe that the shopkeeper was a crook who had deliberately diddled him out of his money.

Suddenly, a strange tinkling-clinking came from across the room, followed by a plopping sound. Peter sat up and frowned. What was that? He switched on his bedside light. There it was again – the same strange noise. And it seemed to be coming from his chair over by the window. Over the back of the chair were the jumper and the pair of trousers Peter had worn on Christmas Eve. That strange noise couldn't be coming from them – could it? Swallowing hard, Peter got up and tiptoed across to the chair.

Tinkle! Clinkle! Plop!

There it was again! Peter took a deep breath, counted to three, then quickly pulled the chair to one side. More money fell out of his trouser pockets and plopped on to the carpet. Peter's eyes goggled! Where had all that money come from? He scooped up the money on the floor, then picked up his trousers and dug into his pockets. There was more money inside them. He counted it all very carefully. It was the exact amount of money he had paid for the Christmas crackers...

Peter sat down on his bed and stared down at the money in his hand. What was going on? He shook his head and looked around the room hoping for some clue. Had Mum and Dad done it? Had they put the money in his pockets to make up for him losing his money in The Christmas Shop? But they didn't know exactly how much he'd paid for the crackers. And now here he was, with the exact same coins in his hand.

Then something else caught his eye. There on his bed-side table, were all the Christmas cards he'd received from his friends. At the front was the card he'd got from his best friend Andy. Peter gasped and stared so hard, his eyes began to ache. The face on the card... Peter had seen that face before – in The Christmas Shop.

The shopkeeper and Father Christmas were one and the same person... Peter picked up the card and studied it. The shopkeeper *was* Father Christmas. Peter was sure of it. And that would explain how he'd got his money back. Which meant only one thing... The Christmas crackers *were* magic after all.

"Thank you," Peter whispered to the Christmas card. And he was sure that on the card, the smiling face of Father Christmas winked at him.

hen Santa Claus Comes
Anon

A good time is coming, I wish it were here,
The very best time in the whole of the year;
I'm counting each day on my fingers and thumbs,
The weeks that must pass before Santa Claus comes.

Then when the first snowflakes begin to come down,
And the wind whistles sharp and the branches are brown,
I'll not mind the cold, though my fingers it numbs,
For it brings the time nearer when Santa Claus comes.

See *Amid* The *Winter's* Snow

Words by **Edward Caswall**   *Music by* **John Goss**

Gently, not too fast

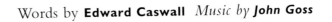

See a-mid the win-ter's snow, born for us on earth be-low.

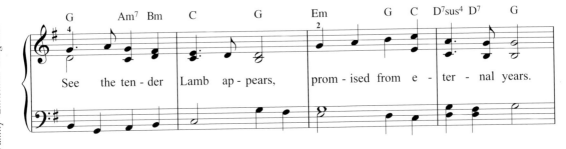

See the ten-der Lamb ap-pears, prom-ised from e-ter-nal years.

Hail, thou ev - er - bless - ed morn; hail, re - demp-tion's hap - py dawn!

Sing through all Je - ru - sa - lem, Christ is born in Beth - le - hem.

2 Lo, within a manger lies
He who built the starry skies;
He who, throned in heights sublime,
Sits amid the cherubim.
Hail, thou ever-blessed morn…

3 Say, ye holy shepherds, say,
What your joyful news today?
Wherefore have ye left your sheep
On the lonely mountain steep?
Hail, thou ever-blessed morn…

4 'As we watched at dead of night,
Lo, we saw a wondrous light;
Angels, singing peace on earth,
Told us of the Saviour's birth.'
Hail, thou ever-blessed morn…

5 Sacred infant, all divine,
What a tender love was thine,
Thus to come from highest bliss,
Down to such a world as this!
Hail, thou ever-blessed morn…

6 Virgin mother, Mary blest,
By the joys that fill thy breast,
Pray for us, that we may prove
Worthy of the Saviour's love.
Hail, thou ever-blessed morn…

Silent *Night*

Words by **Joseph Mohr** *Music by* **Franz Grüber**

Si - lent night, ho - ly night. All is

calm, all is bright, round yon vir - gin

moth - er and child, ho - ly in - fant, so ten - der and

mild, sleep in hea - ven - ly peace,

sleep___ in hea - ven - ly peace.___

2 Silent night, holy night.
Shepherds quake at the sight,
Glories stream from heaven afar,
Heav'nly hosts sing alleluia:
Christ, the Saviour is born,
Christ, the Saviour is born.

3 Silent night, holy night.
Son of God, love's pure light,
Radiant beams from thy holy face,
With the dawn of redeeming grace:
Jesus, Lord, at thy birth,
Jesus, Lord, at thy birth.

Sussex *Carol*

Traditional

Brightly

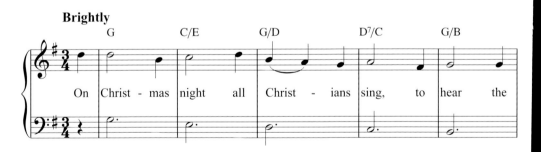

On Christ - mas night all Christ - ians sing, to hear the

news___ the an - gels bring. On Christ - mas night all

Family Christmas Songbook

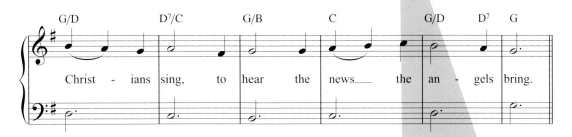

Christ - ians sing, to hear the news___ the an - gels bring.

News of great joy,___ news of___ great mirth,___

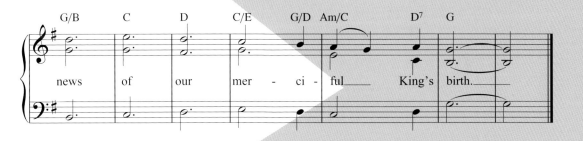

news of our mer - ci - ful___ King's birth.___

Then why should men on earth be so sad,
Since our redeemer made us glad.

2 Then why should men on earth be so sad,
Since our redeemer made us glad.
When from our sin he set us free,
All for to gain our liberty?

All out of darkness we have light,
Which made the angels sing this night:

3 All out of darkness we have light,
Which made the angels sing this night:
"Glory to God and peace to men,
Now and forever more, Amen."

We *Three* Kings *Of* Orient *Are*

Words & Music by **John Henry Hopkins**

Smooth and flowing

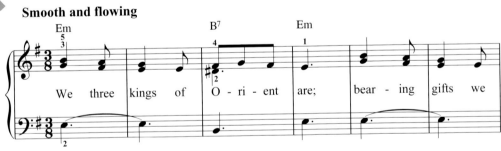

We three kings of O - ri - ent are; bear - ing gifts we

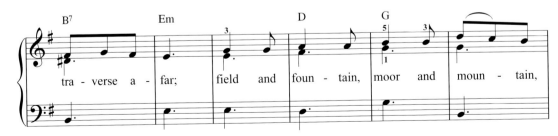

tra - verse a - far; field and foun - tain, moor and moun - tain,

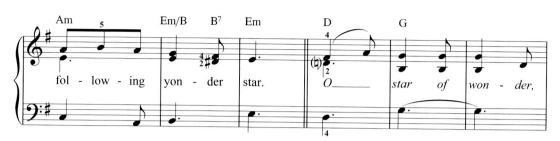

fol - low - ing yon - der star. O_____ star of won - der,

star of night, star with roy - al beau - ty bright, west - ward

lead - ing, still pro - ceed - ing, guide us to thy per - fect light.

2 Born a King on Bethlehem plain,
Gold I bring, to crown him again,
King for ever, ceasing never,
Over us all to reign.
O star of wonder, star of night…

3 Frankincense to offer have I,
Incense owns a Deity nigh,
Prayer and praising, gladly raising,
Worship him, God most high.
O star of wonder, star of night…

4 Myrrh is mine, its bitter perfume
Breathes a life of gathering gloom;
Sorrowing, sighing, bleeding, dying,
Sealed in the stone-cold tomb.
O star of wonder, star of night…

5 Glorious now behold him arise,
King and God and sacrifice;
Alleluia, alleluia,
Earth to heav'n replies.
O star of wonder, star of night…

While *Shepherds* Watched

Words by **Nahum Tate**   *Music* **Traditional**

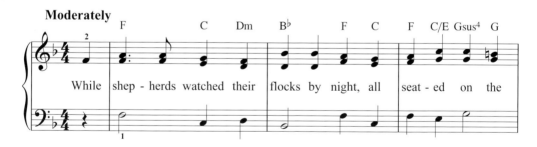

Family Christmas Songbook

2 'Fear not,' said he (for mighty dread
Had seized their troubled mind);
'Glad tidings of great joy I bring
To you and all mankind.'

3 'To you in David's town this day
Is born in David's line
A Saviour, who is Christ the Lord;
And this shall be the sign:'

4 'The heav'nly babe you there shall find
To human view displayed,
All meanly wrapped in swathing bands,
And in a manger laid.'

5 Thus spake the seraph, and forthwith
Appeared a shining throng
Of angels praising God, who thus
Addressed their joyful song:

6 'All glory be to God on high,
And to the earth be peace;
Goodwill henceforth from heav'n to men
Begin and never cease.'

Bethlehem Of Judea

Anon

A little child,
A shining star.
A stable rude,
The door ajar.

Yet in that place,
So crude, folorn,
The Hope of all
The world was born.

O Holy *Night*

By **A Adam**

With movement

O ho - ly night,___ the stars are bright - ly shin - ing, it is the

night of the dear Sa - viour's birth!___ Long lay the

Family Christmas Songbook

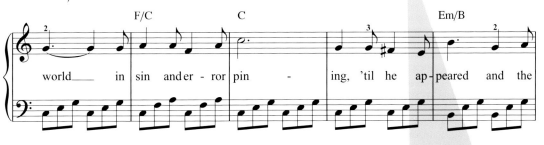

F/C   C   Em/B

world___ in sin and er - ror pin - ing, 'til he ap - peared and the

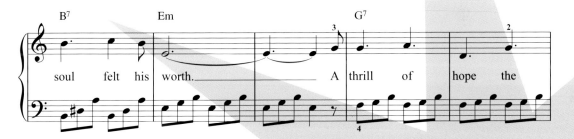

B⁷   Em   G⁷

soul felt his worth.___ A thrill of hope the

C   G⁷   C

wea - ry soul re - joi - ces, for yon - der breaks the new and glo - rious

Am   Em

morn! Fall___ on your knees,___ o

The *Snow-man*
by Mabel *Marlowe*

A snow-man once stood upon a hill, with his face towards the sunset. A very fine snow-man he was, as tall as a soldier, and much fatter. He had two pieces of glass for eyes, and a stone for a nose, and a piece of black wood for a mouth, and in his hand he held a stout, knobbly club. But he had no clothes at all, not even a hat, and the wind on the top of that hill was as bitter as wind could be.

"How cold I am! I am as cold as ice," said the snow-man. "But that red sky looks warm."

So he lifted his feet from the ground, and went tramp, tramp, tramping down the slope towards the setting sun.

Very soon he overtook a gipsy woman, who was wearing a bright red shawl.

"Ha, that looks warm! I must have it," thought the snow-man.

So he went up to the gipsy woman and he said, "Give me that red shawl."

"No, indeed! I cannot spare it on this wintry day," answered the gipsy. "I am cold enough as it is."

"Cold?" shouted the snow-man in a very growlish voice. "Are you as cold as I am, I wonder? Are you cold inside as well as outside? Are you made of ice, through and through and through?"

"No, I suppose not," mumbled the gipsy, who was getting hot with fright.

"Then give me your red shawl this moment, or I shall strike you with my stout, knobbly club."

Then the gipsy took off her red shawl, grumbling all the time, and gave it to the snow-man. He put it round his shoulders, without a word of thanks, and went tramp, tramp, tramping down the hill. And the shivering gipsy followed behind him.

Presently, the snow-man overtook a ploughboy who was wearing his grandmother's long, red woollen mittens.

"Ha, they look warm! I must have them," thought the snow-man.

So he went up to the ploughboy and he said, "Give me those red woollen mittens."

"No, indeed!" said the ploughboy. "They belong to my grandmother. She lent

them to me because my fingers were so cold."

"Cold?" shouted the snow-man, in a very roarish voice. "Are your fingers as cold as mine, I wonder? Are your hands and arms frozen into ice, through and through and through?"

"No, I suppose not," mumbled the ploughboy.

"Then give me those red mittens, this moment, or I shall strike you with my stout, knobbly club."

So the ploughboy drew off the warm mittens, grumbling all the time, and the snow-man put them on, without a word of thanks. Then he went tramp, tramp, tramping down the hill. And the gipsy and the ploughboy followed him.

After a while he overtook a tame pirate, wearing a pirate's thick red cap, with a tassel dangling down his back.

"Ha! That looks warm! I must have it," said the snow-man.

So he went up to the tame pirate and he said, "Give me that red tassel cap."

"No, indeed!" said the pirate. "A nice cold in the head I should get if I did."

"Cold in the head?" shouted the snow-man, in a very thunderish voice. "Is your head as cold as mine, I wonder? Are your brains made of snow, and your bones solid ice, through and through and through?"

"No, I suppose not," muttered the tame pirate.

"Then give me that red tassel cap, this moment, or I shall set upon you with my stout, knobbly club."

Now the pirate felt very sorry that he had turned tame, but he did not like the look of that knobbly stick, so he gave up his red tassel cap. The snow-man put it on without a word of thanks. Then he went tramp, tramp, tramping down the hill, with the tassel bumping up and down. And the gipsy woman, and the ploughboy, and the tame pirate followed him.

At last he reached the bottom of the hill, where the village school house stood, and there was the village schoolmaster on the doorstep, looking at the sunset. He was smoking a glowing briar pipe, and on his feet were two red velvet slippers.

"Ha! Those look warm! I must have them," said the snow-man.

So he went up to the schoolmaster and said, "Give me those red slippers."

"Certainly, if you want them," said the schoolmaster. "Take them by all means.

It is far too cold today to be tramping about with bare toes," and he stooped and drew off his slippers, and there he stood in some bright red socks, thick and woolly and knitted by hand.

"Ha! Those look warm! Give them to me!" said the snow-man.

"Certainly, if you want them," said the schoolmaster. "But you must come inside. I cannot take my socks off here, in the doorway. Come on to the mat."

So the snow-man stepped inside the doorway, and stood upon the mat.

"Be sharp with those socks. My feet are as cold as solid ice," he grumbled.

"I am sorry to hear that," said the schoolmaster. "But I have a warm red blanket airing over the stove. Come in, sir. Sit on that chair by the fire, sir. Put your cold feet upon this snug red footstool, and let me wrap this red blanket around your legs."

So the snow-man came into the schoolhouse, and sat upon a chair by the glowing fire, and put his feet upon the red footstool, and the schoolmaster wrapped the red blanket round and round and round his legs. (And all this while the gipsy woman, and the ploughboy and the tame pirate were peering in at the window.)

"Are you feeling warmer?" asked the schoolmaster.

"No. I am as cold as an iceberg."

"Come closer to the fire."

So the schoolmaster pushed the chair closer to the fire, but the snow-man gave him not one word of thanks.

"Are you feeling warmer now?"

"No. I am as cold as a stone. My feet feel like icy water."

"Move closer to the fire," said the schoolmaster, and he pushed the chair right against the kerb. "There! Are you warmer now?"

"No, no, no! I am colder than ever. I cannot feel my feet at all; I cannot feel my legs at all; I cannot feel my back at all."

Then the schoolmaster pushed the chair quite close up against the stove.

"Are you warmer now?" he said.

But there was no answer, except a slithery sliding sound, and the drip, drip, drip of black snow-water.

"Dear me!" whispered the snow-man, in a gurgling kind of voice. "I have dropped my stout, knobbly club. My red slippers are floating into the ash-pan. My mittens are

swimming in a little river on the floor. My shawl is gone. My red tassel cap is slipping, slipping away. My head is going... going..."

Splosh! Splash! Gurgle!

"That's the end of him," said the schoolmaster, and he went to fetch the mop.

Then the gipsy woman, and the ploughboy and the tame pirate came in and picked up their things, and wrung them out, and dried them at the stove, and the schoolmaster put his red slippers on the hearth, and hung the red blanket over the back of the chair.

Then he picked up the stout, knobbly club and gave the fire a poke.

Hang Up The Baby's Stocking

Anon

Hang up the baby's stocking! Be sure you don't forget!
The dear little dimpled darling, she never saw Christmas yet!
But I've told her all about it, and she opened her big blue eyes;
And I'm sure she understood it – she looked so funny and wise.

Dear, what a tiny stocking! It doesn't take much to hold
Such little pink toes as baby's away from the frost and cold.
But then, for the baby's Christmas, it will never do at all.
Why! Santa wouldn't be looking for anything half so small.

I know what will do for the baby; I've thought of the very best plan.
I'll borrow a stocking of Grandma's; the longest that ever I can.
And you'll hang it by mine, dear mother, right here in the corner, so!
And leave a letter to Santa, and fasten it on to the toe.

Write – this is the baby's stocking that hangs in the corner here.
You never have seen her, Santa, for she only came this year.
But she's just the blessed'st baby. And now before you go,
Just cram her stocking with goodies, from the top clean down to the toe!